EMOTIONAL HEALING

WORKBOOK

A GUIDED PATH TO EMOTIONAL MATURITY,

CULTIVATING INNER PEACE, AND

EMBODYING EMOTIONAL INTELLIGENCE.

Randy Lyman

For inquiries or bulk orders, contact:
hello@TheThirdElement.com

Cover and interior design by Jenny Leavitt

Published by Third Element Publishing™
ThirdElementPublishing.com

ISBN: 979-8-9924892-4-8

CONTENTS

Feel it. Believe it. Live it.

EMOTIONAL
HEALING
WORKBOOK

Everyone would like to feel better, have more time for fun, and experience more abundance. We all want more of the good things in life and fewer hard times and challenges. This workbook is a step-by-step guide to take you on a path to discovery and healing.

I developed this guide in late 2023 as I was working through my own emotional healing around deservedness and abundance.

The best time to use this guide is when addressing an unanswered desire or issue that you've not been able to resolve to your satisfaction.

The questions will help lead you to and through the thoughts and feelings behind the current situation and allow whatever is causing you to be held back to be released so you can attract the situation or state or mind you are trying to reach.

There are no wrong answers, and you don't have to share what you write with anyone.

I find it works best for me when I write down the first thing that comes to mind without overthinking what might be the best answer. The more we are able to respond spontaneously, the more intuition will step in and help out.

It isn't necessary to fill in each and every answer. If the answer is not coming to you, simply move on to the next question. Just be aware of the questions without answers without judgement as to why.

You can always go back and think your way through it after answering the best you can on the first time through. And, there is always the option of going through the entire list again at a different time. I know I certainly have used this more than once as I worked my way through a challenge or two!

Randy

WHAT IS THE STATE OF OUR MIND AND OUR EMOTIONS?

SECTION 1

We start here by looking at why we picked up this book in the first place. For me, writing this was all about letting go of my belief in lack and a low level of deservedness. Although I had already made a small fortune, I had lost most of it and definitely lost the lifestyle I had become accustomed to. Using this guide for myself has helped me to let go of many of my own limiting beliefs and get back on the path to receiving more abundance.

1 What situations (emotional events) from your past do you remember that are similar to what you are dealing with today?

2 What are you feeling today? (Describe it the best you can)

3 What do you think this feeling might be indicating?

4   What if the interpretation of what you are feeling is correct?

5   Is it possible you will fail?

6   What could that failure lead to?

7 Could any momentary failure ultimately lead to something better in the future?

8 What is a memory from childhood when you felt calm, free, or safe in your body?

9 Who first taught you that your emotions mattered, or that they didn't?

10   **Do you remember when you became aware of your emotions?**

11   **Do you remember when you began to understand your emotions?**

WHAT YOU ARE EXPERIENCING THAT YOU WOULD LIKE TO CHANGE

SECTION 2

We might be looking for something new to come into our life, to remove something that does not serve us, or simply looking to change something that we know can improve. A great way to start making improvement is to become clear about what we would like to see different or better. We always have the option of changing our perspective, to reach for something more, and find more success in all areas of our life.

1 How calm do you feel today? (Circle how you feel, 10 being the most calm) And describe if helpful.

1 2 3 4 5 6 7 8 9 10

2 How happy and content do you feel today? (Circle how you feel, 10 being fully happy and content) And describe if helpful.

1 2 3 4 5 6 7 8 9 10

3 Why are you feeling that way?

2 – WHAT YOU ARE EXPERIENCING THAT YOU WANT TO CHANGE

4 How frustrated or off-center do you feel today? (Circle how you feel, 10 being completely off center) And describe if helpful.

1 2 3 4 5 6 7 8 9 10

5 Why are you feeling that way?

6 What do you want that you don't have?

7 What do you need that you don't have?

8 What are you experiencing that you would rather not?

9 How might changing this situation change your life?

10 When have you successfully created a change in your life before?

11 What helped you do it?

12 Who in your life has inspired you to grow or try again when you wanted to give up?

"Every challenge you face is designed for your growth. Nothing in life is random."

THE STORY OUR MIND MAKES UP AS TO WHY WE ARE WHERE WE ARE

SECTION 3

Regardless of whether challenges in our life are real, or they are only based on what we are worried will become real, it is easier to overcome challenges when we can separate our thoughts about a problem from the problem itself. This section will help you become clearer as to what part of the problem is based on our thoughts and perceptions around the issue. I'm not saying there isn't a real issue that can be fixed or a situation that cannot be improved. I am saying sometimes our minds make up unhelpful stories around the situation based on our past experiences, beliefs, and emotional wounds.

1 **What do you believe about yourself that might be holding you back from accomplishing or achieving what you would like to change, attract, or improve?**

2 **Who did you learn these beliefs from? Or, which experiences in your past led you to take on these beliefs?**

3 **Is it possible your limiting beliefs are not true?**

4 **How would you describe who you are trying to be based on those beliefs in order to impress other people?**

5   **What might help you change your thoughts or heal the emotional wounds you have around those limiting beliefs?**

6   **What story did your family or community teach you about success, love, or worthiness?**

7   **Which of those stories still influence you today?**

8   **Which story are you ready to rewrite?**

THE FEELINGS WE HAVE AND THE STORIES OUR MIND HANGS ON TO

SECTION 4

As long as we are human, we will experience feelings and emotions. Both negative and positive emotions are part of our earthly experience which help guide us to a better life, and they enrich our overall human experience. However, at times emotions from our past surface as feelings in real time and get in the way of living our life to the fullest. Sometimes the thoughts and feelings we have about our situation, related to the underlying emotions, can get in the way of our happiness. This section is designed to uncover the thoughts and feelings that we have the opportunity to work through in order to reach our goals. Although uncovering underlying emotions is also helpful, this section is about becoming more aware of the thoughts and feelings we are experiencing around the situation that we would like to change without the need to dig into emotions.

1 **What is happening in your life that is bothering you?**

2 **What feelings might you be avoiding right now?**

3 **Why might you be avoiding those feelings?**

4   What are you feeling that you would rather not be feeling right now?

5   What belief about yourself causes the most pain?

6   Do you have any destructive behaviors you continue to repeat? If so, what are they?

7 Do you sometimes make other people more important than yourself? If so, why?

8 What part of yourself have you silenced to keep the peace with others?

9 Is there anything wrong with considering yourself more important than other people?

10 If so, where or who did you learn that from?

11 Could it be helpful to let go of that way of seeing things? Why or why not?

12 What identity have you outgrown but still cling to out of habit or safety?

13 What would help you start letting go of that way of thinking?

14 Could it be helpful to let go of that way of seeing things?

15 What would help you start letting go of that way of thinking?

4 - THE STORIES OUR MIND HANGS ON TO

16 What past experience taught you that you were stronger than you thought?

17 When was a time you truly felt someone's compassion towards you?

THE EMOTIONS BENEATH
OUR FEELINGS

SECTION 5

When we feel something in our body, it is either our body letting us know we have a physical challenge to attend to, something wonderful to enjoy, or feelings related to our emotions ready to be experienced whether we like it or not. Although we make up stories in our mind around our emotions, the only way we can feel our emotions is through our physical body. This section provides an opportunity to dig deeper and embrace the feelings on the surface in a way that can lead us to the underlying emotions that create the feelings we experience in our body.

1   What do you feel when thinking about, or reaching for, your goal?

2   Where in your body are you feeling it? (e.g., neck, head, shoulders, heart, stomach)

3   Describe the uncomfortable feelings in detail the best you can.

4 **Can you remember a time you felt completely at peace in your body?**

5 **What was happening around you?**

6 **What does it feel like when you need to rest and or reset?**

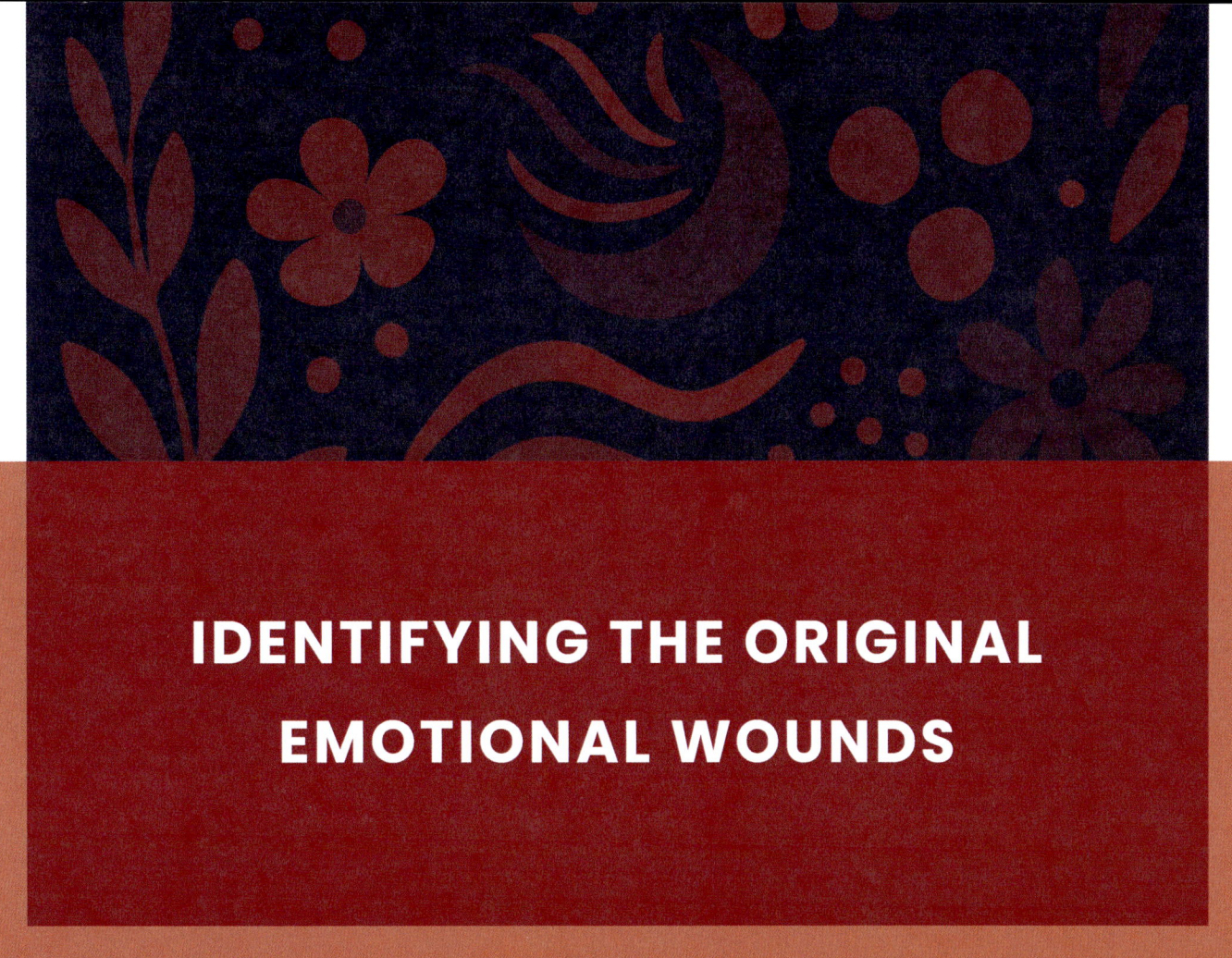

IDENTIFYING THE ORIGINAL EMOTIONAL WOUNDS

SECTION 6

Whenever we have emotions from the past that are negatively affecting our reality today, we have the opportunity to identify them and heal them so they can be released and no longer have a negative impact on our daily life. This section is about digging one level deeper than the feeling itself. This is about getting all the way back to the original event that caused the emotional wound that is still influencing our life today.

1 What did you not accomplish or receive in the past that might be the result of the way others interacted with you, or ignored you?

2 Is it possible you would be in a different position today if events of the past were different?

3 What does it feel like today when you think of the way recent events have negatively impacted your life? Describe your thoughts and feelings around those challenges you are facing today.

4 Was there a time in your past that you experienced something similar to what you are experiencing today? Does the current challenge remind you of anything from the past, even if it was not exactly the same as what you are experiencing today? Write everything down that comes to mind.

5 Are the negative feelings you are experiencing today directed at others, or at yourself?

6 Is there anything else you are feeling now that might be related to something you experienced in the past?

7 Are you able to put pictures or words to the memories brought up by what you are feeling and experiencing today? What are they?

8 Is there anything you didn't accomplish or receive in the past that might be due to you being less important than someone or something else?

9 Do you sometimes make others more important than yourself?

10 What might happen if you make your wants and needs more important than other people's?

11 Is there anything wrong with putting your own needs ahead of others'?

12 Where or when did you learn that you should make others more important than yourself?

13 How does this affect how you take care of yourself in the world?

14 Is it possible you have negative thoughts or feelings about yourself or others? And if so, can you articulate what you are thinking or feeling?

15 Does any good come to me by having these thoughts?

16 Where did you learn these thoughts from?

17 How can you change or replace these thoughts?

18 What negative thoughts do you have about your body?

19 Where did you learn these thoughts from?

20 How can you change or replace these thoughts?

21   What negative thoughts do you have about your family?

22   Do these negative thoughts help you?

23   Where did you think you might have learned these ideas from?

24 Why did you listen to those who taught you to think this way?

25 Can you change or replace these thoughts? And if so, how?

26 What negative thoughts do you have about your workplace?

27 From whom did you learn your beliefs about working environments?

28 Why did you listen to them?

29 What good comes from these thoughts?

30 Is there any reason to hold on to those beliefs today?

31 What can be gained by letting these thoughts and beliefs go?

32 How can you let go of and replace those old beliefs?

33 When you think back on your childhood, what moments shaped how you handle pain?

34 What did you learn from those moments?

35 When did you learn how to be strong and vulnerable at the same time?

HEALING AND RELEASING THE OLD EMOTIONAL WOUNDS

SECTION 7

Although we usually find a way to ignore or bury the feelings of our old emotional wounds, the only way to move past them and let them go forever is to be bold enough to dive back in and feel them completely. The process of reactivating and healing old emotional wounds is a bit different for each of us. However, whatever works to get us back to the original pain and allows us to dive in without holding back is what is necessary for full release. Once we are able to feel the old emotions completely, they leave us forever. If there is something that works for you, continue using it. We simply have to feel it in its entirety without the need for understanding or explanations. Once it has been felt completely, it is gone like gasoline that can only be burned once. In its place comes the love of the Universe to fill up the space within us that the wound used to occupy.

1 What from your past (or present) might be influencing your mood today?

2 If you had a choice, what would you like your mood to be today?

3 Who decides your mood each moment of every day?

4 How can you move toward being in a better mood or having a better outlook on life today?

7 – HEALING AND RELEASING THE OLD EMOTIONAL WOUNDS

5   When have you faced something difficult and felt lighter on the other side?

6   What part of your story are you most proud of healing or surviving?

"Every experience, no matter how painful, is an opportunity to reconnect with your divine self."

FINDING FORGIVENESS

SECTION 8

At one time or another, we all experience wrongdoing by someone or something outside of ourselves. This is a big part of the human experience and there really is no way around it. However, we can work toward seeing the possible positive outcome from our challenging experiences after we are able to move through the process of healing the associated emotional wounds.

Even if you are not yet aware of it, you are already on the path to healing.

1   Do you feel any anger or resentment toward those who have misguided you or done harm to you? If so, write them down.

2   What does that feel like in your mind, body, or emotions?

3   Any idea why you have these feelings?

4 Can you forgive yourself for allowing those things to happen to you?

5 What can you do or think to help yourself understand what you might have gained from the experience and work toward forgiving yourself?

6 What might help you to work toward forgiving Divine Source for allowing it to happen?

7 What might help you work toward forgiving those who did you wrong?

8 What have you forgiven others for, but haven't forgiven yourself for yet?

9 What's getting in the way of helping you to forgive others?

10 What might help you get to the root emotion?

11 What can help you heal the root emotion now?

12 What might be keeping you from healing those emotional wounds from the past?

13 What beliefs might be keeping you from forgiving and healing now?

14 Where could you have learned those beliefs from?

15 Are you ready to let go of those limiting beliefs?

16 What might help you to let go of or replace any beliefs that are not serving you?

17 Can you recall a time someone forgave you when you didn't expect it?

18 What did that forgiveness teach you about love or humility?

SEEING CHALLENGES AND WRONGDOINGS AS GIFTS

SECTION 9

It is my belief that nothing in our life is random and everything is for our learning and growth. I believe there is something positive to be found in every situation; even the horrific ones. Even if you don't believe that, I'm asking you to suspend your disbelief for a moment as you consider the questions in this section.

We are always exactly where we are meant to be for our growth & healing.

1 What might you have gained from the experiences of being misled or wronged?

2 What is another way to look at and approach the challenges you are facing that will bring better results? What does that look like?

3   **What challenge from your past helped you grow into who you are now?**

4   **What qualities did you develop through hardship that you now appreciate?**

FINDING GRATITUDE FOR THE LESSONS/GIFTS WE EXPERIENCE

SECTION 10

The fastest way for many to connect with the love of the Universe and find a way to forgive is through gratitude. There are so many challenges in life, and at the same time there are so many things we can be grateful for. If we are able to see the lessons in the challenges we encounter, we can often find a way to be grateful for those lessons and whatever positive experiences might have come through navigating the challenges. Once we are able to find a reason to have gratitude for the situations, it then becomes a lot easier for us to forgive. And when we are able to truly forgive, we no longer have the need for the same lessons again.

1 Are you able to think of anything positive you experienced due to the challenge? If so, write it below.

2 Is there any reason to be thankful for the lesson(s)?

3 If it feels right to you, write out "I am thankful now for the lessons I experienced due to the wrongdoings I experienced" or something similar that works for you.

4 What does it feel like to have gratitude for the challenge you experienced?

5   What three moments in your past are you now grateful for?

6   Who or what has remained a constant positive influence through your life's ups and downs?

7   What have you learned from having that consistency?

REALIZING IT IS US WHO IS IN CONTROL OF OUR LIFE

SECTION 11

As much as I want to blame the world for the challenges I face, and try to get others to change, I always come back to the realization that it is me who is ultimately in charge of my life. That is a tough pill to swallow at times, but it always leads me to a better place and empowers me to find solutions without the need to change others. And, after 60 years of trying to get other people to change so my life improves, I have come to know that is simply too much to ask. We all want to blame others from time to time; myself included. However, I believe each of us has the power to improve our lives through our thoughts, actions, and by becoming aware of, and working with, our emotions.

1 Do you have any reason to blame others for what you experienced?

2 Do those reasons or does that blame help you?

3 Is it possible this challenge was created for you in order to help you learn, or to help you feel old emotional wounds that are ready to be reactivated, felt completely, and released?

4   Where or from who did you learn that others are to blame for your challenges?

5   Are you open-minded and willing to consider changing your thoughts toward blame?

6   If not, why might you be trying to hang on to your old beliefs?

7 What do you think you could change within yourself that would help you gain more control over your life?

8 Are you ready and willing to make those changes? If not, why might you be hesitant to change?

9 How do those things you are hanging onto serve you?

10 When have you taken charge of your life, even in small ways?

11 What strengths do you now see in yourself that you didn't recognize before?

"We are the creator of our realities, and the power to change our lives for the better depends on our ability to understand and embrace our emotions."

11 - REALIZING IT IS US WHO IS IN CONTROL OF OUR LIFE

CHANGING OUR OUTLOOK AND APPROACH TO LIFE AND OUR CHALLENGES

SECTION 12

I realize we cannot predict what is coming our way most of the time. However, we can always choose how we react to whatever does come our way. For me, remembering the love of Divine Source is always with me gets me through even life's biggest challenges as long as I also ask for help and keep an open mind as to what I am going to encounter along the path to a lasting solution. It also helps to *surrender* to receiving Divine Source's guidance and assistance as we navigate life's challenges.

1 Consider writing out something like "I know that my life is better now and will continue to improve a little bit every day" or whatever feels right to you.

2 What thoughts and feelings came up when writing out the affirmation above?

3 Consider writing out something like "I trust the Universe is guiding me to peace, a solution, and acceptance of His timing" in your own words.

4 What thoughts and feelings come up when thinking about trusting the Universe to support you?

5 What values matter most to you today than they did five years ago?

6 What might you think or do differently to improve your attitude and outlook on life?

7 What might help you keep moving forward in a positive direction even in the face of adversity?

8 Recall a situation that once felt hopeless, what helped you see it differently?

9 If fear disappeared for 24 hours, what decision would you make?

10 Where are you being invited to step into more truth, courage, and compassion?

11 What simple daily practice or mindset keeps you anchored in hope and possibility?

CREATING A GREAT LIFE THROUGH OUR THOUGHTS, ACTIONS, EMOTIONS

SECTION 13

Life will always bring us unexpected turns, yet the quality of our experience depends on how we choose to respond. By aligning our thoughts, actions, and emotions, we unlock our ability to create a great life from the inside out. This section guides you to practice daily alignment, and lean into affirmations that invite clarity and freedom. With each conscious choice, we step closer to living a life shaped not by fear or old patterns, but by intention, love, and trust in the guidance always available to us.

1 Write out something such as "I take steps every day to improve my thoughts and I allow my emotions to flow through me freely"?

2 What steps can you take to be more in touch with your emotions at all times?

3 If you are hesitant to take those steps, why are you hesitant?

4 What does a "great life" mean to you now?

5 How has that vision evolved?

6 Where have you underestimated your strength?

7 Which daily habits, relationships, or mindsets already reflect the life you're creating?

8 What part of you are you ready to reclaim without apology?

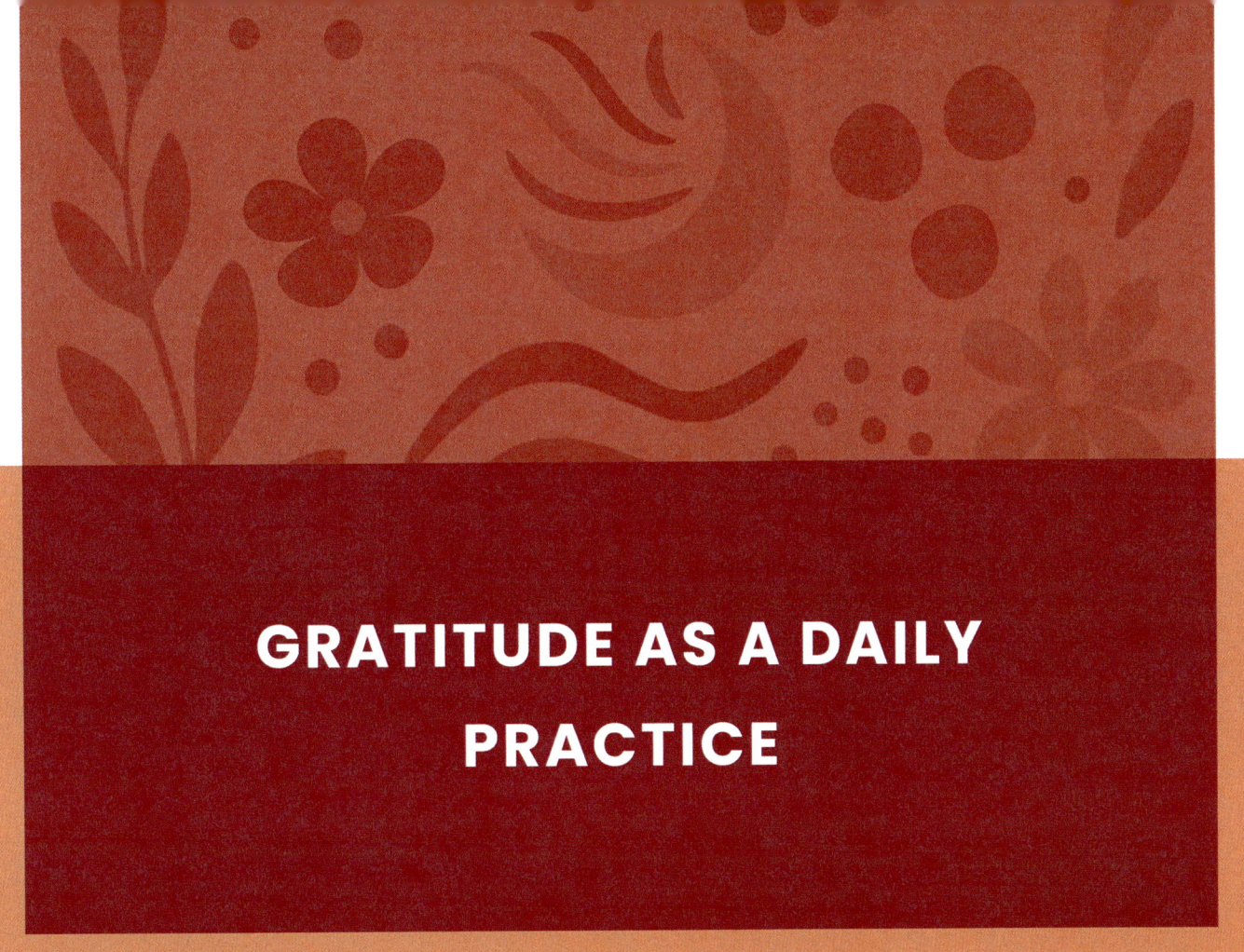

GRATITUDE AS A DAILY PRACTICE

SECTION 14

The best way to attract more experiences to be grateful for is to be grateful for what we have already experienced. Although this is a very short section, it doesn't need to be long in order to be powerful. Gratitude is like a cheat code and the Law of Attraction sort of hides in the shadows, waiting for us to slow down enough to think about, AND FEEL, anything at all we are grateful for. It is so easy to shift our energy and mood to a more positive place when we take a few minutes to consider all that is good in our life and the world. Living in a state of grace at all times is something I continue to aspire to, but even brief moments of genuine gratitude have the power to recalibrate everything. When we pause to truly feel thankful, we step into alignment with the frequency of abundance, and from that place, life begins to respond in ways we never expected.

1 Write out something such "Every day I give thanks to Source for leading down the road that best serves me and for all the great people and situations being brought into my life."?

2 What situations in the past remind you of the abundance you have already experienced?

3 Write a positive statement about your current state of abundance.

4 What are five small things, people, moments, and sensations, that you can appreciate right now?

5 How might your life feel different if gratitude became your default each day?

YOUR JOURNEY DOESN'T END HERE.

You've just done some very powerful work. You've faced what most people spend a lifetime avoiding. That deserves acknowledgment. Take a breath. Feel into what has shifted.

THE PORTAL

This portal includes guided practices that bring you back into presence & alignment in just minutes. Each practice helps to release old patterns and step forward with clarity and peace.

THE BOOK

This book expands on what you've just experienced, weaving together story, science, and spirit to explain how thoughts, actions, and emotions work together. This is the missing piece to creating a life you truly love.

Whether continuing with the book, the portal, or simply revisiting this workbook, know this: healing is not about fixing yourself. **It's about remembering who you are.**

TAKE SOME TIME TO LET IT ALL SINK IN

Whenever we go through change or emotional growth, it takes time for our mind and body to catch up. It always helps me to meditate or spend time walking in nature as much as possible during the integration process.

I hope this workbook has been as helpful for you as it has been for me. Please send me your questions, comments, or suggestions by scanning the QR code below.

May all of your dreams and desires come true!

Blessings,

Randy

STAY IN TOUCH

Randy
hello@thethirdelement.com
RandyLyman.com

"If we are not willing to own our emotional issues they will own us."

NOTES

Made in the USA
Middletown, DE
27 February 2026

29140747R00051